MW01205552

for

_____

from

_____

*God heals the brokenhearted
and binds up their wounds.*

—Psalm 147:3 (NIV)

Biblica Publishing
We welcome your questions and comments.

USA   1820 Jet Stream Drive, Colorado Springs, CO 80921
             www.Biblica.com

God's Promises on Healing
ISBN 978-1-934068-91-5

Livingstone project staff includes Andy Culbertson, Linda Taylor, Joan
Guest, Everett O'Bryan. Interior design by Lindsay Galvin and Larry
Taylor.

Published in 2008 by Authentic.

A catalog record for this book is available from the Library of Congress.

Printed in the United States of America

GOD'S PROMISES

on Healing

CONTENTS

OUR CARING

God

I called on Your name, O Lord, from the lowest pit. You have heard my voice: "Do not hide Your ear from my sighing, from my cry for help." You drew near on the day I called on You, and said, "Do not fear!"

—Lamentations 3:55–57 (NKJV)

LORD, You have heard the desire of the humble; You will prepare their heart; You will cause Your ear to hear.
—*Psalm 10:17 (NKJV)*

As for me, I look to the LORD for help. I wait confidently for God to save me, and my God will certainly hear me.
—*Micah 7:7 (NLT)*

Then he said to me, "Do not fear, Daniel, for from the first day that you set your heart to understand, and to humble yourself before your God, your words were heard; and I have come because of your words."
—*Daniel 10:12 (NKJV)*

For he will deliver the needy who cry out, the afflicted who have no one to help.

—*Psalm 72:12 (NIV)*

The Lord helps poor people who have troubles. The Lord is not ashamed of them. He doesn't hate them. If people call to the Lord for help, he will not hide from them.

—*Psalm 22:24 (ERV)*

I called to the Lord, and he heard me. He heard my cries.

—*Psalm 40:1 (ERV)*

Is he deaf—the one who made your ears? Is he blind—the one who formed your eyes? . . . The LORD will not reject his people; he will not abandon his special possession.

—*Psalm 94:9, 14 (NLT)*

So Solomon finished building the Lord's temple and his own palace. Solomon built all the things that he wanted to build. Then the Lord appeared to Solomon again, just as he had done before in the town of Gibeon. The Lord said to him: "I heard your prayer. I heard the things that you asked me to do. You built this temple. And I have made it a holy place. So I will be honored there forever. I will watch over it and think of it always."

—*1 Kings 9:1–3 (ERV)*

Surely the arm of the LORD is not too short to save, nor his ear too dull to hear.

—*Isaiah 59:1 (NIV)*

The eyes of the LORD are on the righteous, and His ears are open to their cry.

—*Psalm 34:15 (NKJV)*

When the LORD saw that he had gone over to look, God called to him from within the bush, "Moses! Moses!"

And Moses said, "Here I am."

"Do not come any closer," God said. "Take off your sandals, for the place where you are standing is holy ground." Then he said, "I am the God of your father, the God of Abraham, the God of Isaac and the God of Jacob." At this, Moses hid his face, because he was afraid to look at God.

The LORD said, "I have indeed seen the misery of my people in Egypt. I have heard them crying out because of their slave drivers, and I am concerned about their suffering."

—*Exodus 3:4–7 (NIV)*

Most of those who came from Ephraim, Manasseh, Issachar, and Zebulun had not purified themselves. But King Hezekiah prayed for them, and they were allowed to eat the Passover meal anyway, even though this was contrary to the requirements of the Law. For Hezekiah said, "May the LORD, who is good, pardon those who decide to follow the LORD, the God of their ancestors, even though they are not properly cleansed for the ceremony." And the LORD listened to Hezekiah's prayer and healed the people.

—*2 Chronicles 30:18–20 (NLT)*

But you see the trouble and grief they cause. You take note of it and punish them. The helpless put their trust in you. You defend the orphans.

—*Psalm 10:14 (NLT)*

Because your heart was responsive and you humbled yourself before God when you heard what he spoke against this place and its people, and because you humbled yourself before me and tore your robes and wept in my presence, I have heard you, declares the LORD.
—*2 Chronicles 34:27 (NIV)*

Why are you cast down, O my soul?
And why are you disquieted within me?
Hope in God; for I shall yet praise Him,
the help of my countenance and my
God.

> —*Psalm 42:11 (NKJV)*

Praise the Lord; praise God our savior!
For each day he carries us in his arms.

> —*Psalm 68:19 (NLT)*

Forget the former things; do not dwell
on the past. See, I am doing a new
thing! Now it springs up; do you not
perceive it? I am making a way in the
desert and streams in the wasteland.

> —*Isaiah 43:18–19 (NIV)*

For I know the thoughts that I think toward you, says the LORD, thoughts of peace and not of evil, to give you a future and a hope. Then you will call upon Me and go and pray to Me, and I will listen to you. And you will seek Me and find Me, when you search for Me with all your heart.

—*Jeremiah 29:11–13 (NKJV)*

But then I think of something else, then I have hope. What I think of is this: The Lord's love and kindness never ends. His compassion never ends.

—*Lamentations 3:21–22 (ERV)*

Know also that wisdom is sweet to your soul; if you find it, there is a future hope for you, and your hope will not be cut off.

—*Proverbs 24:14 (NIV)*

Because of our faith, Christ has brought us into this place of undeserved privilege where we now stand, and we confidently and joyfully look forward to sharing God's glory. We can rejoice, too, when we run into problems and trials, for we know that they help us develop endurance. And endurance develops strength of character, and character strengthens our confident hope of salvation. And this hope will not lead to disappointment. For we know how dearly God loves us, because he has given us the Holy Spirit to fill our hearts with his love.

—Romans 5:2–5 (NLT)

The LORD is good to those who depend on him, to those who search for him. So it is good to wait quietly for salvation from the LORD.

—Lamentations 3:25–26 (NLT)

Now may the God of hope fill you with all joy and peace in believing, that you may abound in hope by the power of the Holy Spirit.
—*Romans 15:13 (NKJV)*

Be strong and brave, all of you people that are waiting for the Lord's help!
—*Psalm 31:24 (ERV)*

God IS YOUR PROTECTOR

The Lord will lead his people like a shepherd leads sheep. The Lord will use his arm (power) and gather his sheep together. The Lord will pick up the little sheep and hold them in his arms. Their mothers will walk beside him.

—*Isaiah 40:11 (ERV)*

You whom I have taken from the ends of the earth, and called from its farthest regions, and said to you, "You are My servant, I have chosen you and have not cast you away: Fear not, for I am with you; be not dismayed, for I am your God. I will strengthen you, yes, I will help you, I will uphold you with My righteous right hand."

—*Isaiah 41:9–10 (NKJV)*

He saves and protects good, honest people. He protects people who are fair to other people. He guards his holy people.

—*Proverbs 2:7–8 (ERV)*

Those who fear the LORD are secure; he will be a refuge for their children.

—*Proverbs 14:26 (NLT)*

The angel of the LORD encamps around those who fear him, and he delivers them.

—*Psalm 34:7 (NIV)*

Give heed to the voice of my cry, my King and my God, for to You I will pray.

—*Psalm 5:2 (NKJV)*

If I rise on the wings of the dawn, if I settle on the far side of the sea, even there your hand will guide me, your right hand will hold me fast.

—*Psalm 139:9–10 (NIV)*

But the Lord says: "Bad people stole from the poor people. They took things from helpless people. But now I will stand and defend those weary (tired) people."

—*Psalm 12:5 (ERV)*

As for God, His way is perfect; the word of the LORD is proven; He is a shield to all who trust in Him. "For who is God, except the LORD? And who is a rock, except our God?"

—*2 Samuel 22:31–32 (NKJV)*

The LORD is good, a refuge in times of trouble. He cares for those who trust in him.

—*Nahum 1:7 (NIV)*

God's way is perfect. All the LORD'S promises prove true. He is a shield for all who look to him for protection.

—*Psalm 18:30 (NLT)*

My enemies were trying to kill me! The ropes of death were all around me. I was caught in a flood carrying me to that place of death. Ropes of the grave were all around me. Traps of death lay before me. Trapped, I called to the Lord for help. Yes, I called to my God. God was in his temple. He heard my voice. He heard my cry for help.

—Psalm 18:4–6 (ERV)

The Lord saves good people. When good people have troubles, the Lord is their strength.

—Psalm 37:39 (ERV)

The LORD directs the steps of the godly. He delights in every detail of their lives. Though they stumble, they will never fall, for the LORD holds them by the hand.

—Psalm 37:23–24 (NLT)

Do not forsake her, and she will preserve you; love her, and she will keep you.

     —Proverbs 4:6 (NKJV)

Cast your cares on the LORD and he will sustain you; he will never let the righteous fall.

     —Psalm 55:22 (NIV)

Blessed is he who has regard for the weak; the LORD delivers him in times of trouble. The LORD will protect him and preserve his life; he will bless him in the land and not surrender him to the desire of his foes. The LORD will sustain him on his sickbed and restore him from his bed of illness.

     —Psalm 41:1–3 (NIV)

God IS YOUR COMFORT

I always remember your wise decisions.
Lord, your wise decisions comfort me.
  —*Psalm 119:52 (ERV)*

But now, thus says the LORD, who
created you, O Jacob, and He who
formed you, O Israel: "Fear not, for I
have redeemed you; I have called you
by your name; you are Mine. When
you pass through the waters, I will
be with you; and through the rivers,
they shall not overflow you. When you
walk through the fire, you shall not be
burned, nor shall the flame scorch you.
For I am the LORD your God, the Holy
One of Israel, your Savior; I gave Egypt
for your ransom, Ethiopia and Seba in
your place."
  —*Isaiah 43:1–3 (NKJV)*

How precious is Your lovingkindness, O God! Therefore the children of men put their trust under the shadow of Your wings.

—*Psalm 36:7 (NKJV)*

What great blessings there are for the people that are sad now! God will comfort them.

—*Matthew 5:4 (ERV)*

Praise be to the God and Father of our Lord Jesus Christ, the Father of compassion and the God of all comfort, who comforts us in all our troubles, so that we can comfort those in any trouble with the comfort we ourselves have received from God.

—*2 Corinthians 1:3–4 (NIV)*

Even though I walk through the valley of the shadow of death, I will fear no evil, for you are with me; your rod and your staff, they comfort me.

—*Psalm 23:4 (NIV)*

Sing, O heavens! Be joyful, O earth!
And break out in singing, O mountains!
For the LORD has comforted His people,
and will have mercy on His afflicted.
　　　—Isaiah 49:13 (NKJV)

I will comfort you there in Jerusalem as
a mother comforts her child.
　　　—Isaiah 66:13 (NLT)

"I saw where Israel went. So, I will heal
(forgive) him. I will comfort him and say
words to make him feel better. Then he
and his people will not feel sad. I will
teach them a new word: 'Peace.' I will
give peace to the people near me and to
the people that are far away. I will heal
(forgive) those people!" The Lord himself
said these things.
　　　—Isaiah 57:18–19 (ERV)

Be my rock of safety where I can always hide. Give the order to save me, for you are my rock and my fortress.

—*Psalm 71:3 (NLT)*

God, give me a sign to show that you will help me. My enemies will see that sign, and they will be disappointed. That will show that you heard my prayer and that you will help me.

—*Psalm 86:17 (ERV)*

God IS YOUR GUIDE

For this is God, our God forever and ever; He will be our guide even to death.
—*Psalm 48:14 (NKJV)*

Trust in the LORD with all your heart; do not depend on your own understanding. Seek his will in all you do, and he will show you which path to take.
—*Proverbs 3:5–6 (NLT)*

And the LORD went before them by day in a pillar of cloud to lead the way, and by night in a pillar of fire to give them light, so as to go by day and night. He did not take away the pillar of cloud by day or the pillar of fire by night from before the people.
—*Exodus 13:21–22 (NKJV)*

The LORD will guide you always; he will satisfy your needs in a sun-scorched land and will strengthen your frame. You will be like a well-watered garden, like a spring whose waters never fail.

—Isaiah 58:11 (NIV)

Lord, if I go east where the sun rises, you are there. If I go west to the sea, you are there. Even there your right hand holds me, and you lead me by the hand.

—Psalm 139:9–10 (ERV)

He restores my soul. He guides me in paths of righteousness for his name's sake.

—Psalm 23:3 (NIV)

You will show me the path of life; in Your presence is fullness of joy; at Your right hand are pleasures forevermore.

—Psalm 16:11 (NKJV)

Tears of joy will stream down their faces, and I will lead them home with great care. They will walk beside quiet streams and on smooth paths where they will not stumble. For I am Israel's father, and Ephraim is my oldest child.
—*Jeremiah 31:9 (NLT)*

They will neither hunger nor thirst, nor will the desert heat or the sun beat upon them. He who has compassion on them will guide them and lead them beside springs of water. . . .

Shout for joy, O heavens; rejoice, O earth; burst into song, O mountains! For the LORD comforts his people and will have compassion on his afflicted ones.
—*Isaiah 49:10, 13 (NIV)*

With your unfailing love you lead the people you have redeemed. In your might, you guide them to your sacred home.

—*Exodus 15:13 (NLT)*

Then I will lead the blind people in a way they never knew. I will lead the blind people to places they have never been before. I will change darkness into light for them. And I will make the rough ground smooth. I will do the things I promised! And I will not leave my people.

—*Isaiah 42:16 (ERV)*

But when the Spirit of truth comes, he will lead you into all truth. The Spirit of truth will not speak his own words. He will speak only what he hears. He will tell you the things that will happen.

—*John 16:13 (ERV)*

God IS YOUR CONFIDENCE

The LORD is my light and my salvation—so why should I be afraid? The LORD is my fortress, protecting me from danger, so why should I tremble? . . . Though a mighty army surrounds me, my heart will not be afraid. Even if I am attacked, I will remain confident.
> —*Psalm 27:1, 3 (NLT)*

Blessed is the man who trusts in the LORD, and whose hope is the LORD.
> —*Jeremiah 17:7 (NKJV)*

"Though the mountains be shaken and the hills be removed, yet my unfailing love for you will not be shaken nor my covenant of peace be removed," says the LORD, who has compassion on you.
> —*Isaiah 54:10 (NIV)*

The LORD also will be a refuge for the oppressed, a refuge in times of trouble.

—Psalm 9:9 (NKJV)

Lord, I trusted in your love to help me. You saved me and made me happy! I sing a happy song to the Lord because he did good things for me.

—Psalm 13:5–6 (ERV)

People who know your name should trust you. Lord, if people come to you, you will not leave them without help.

—Psalm 9:10 (ERV)

I am praying to you because I know you will answer, O God. Bend down and listen as I pray.

—Psalm 17:6 (NLT)

This is the confidence we have in approaching God: that if we ask anything according to his will, he hears us.

—1 John 5:14 (NIV)

My Master, you are my hope. I have trusted you since I was a young boy.
—*Psalm 71:5 (ERV)*

For the LORD will be your confidence, and will keep your foot from being caught.
—*Proverbs 3:26 (NKJV)*

So we can say with confidence, "The LORD is my helper, so I will have no fear. What can mere people do to me?"
—*Hebrews 13:6 (NLT)*

God saves me. I trust him. I am not afraid. He saves me. The Lord YAH is my strength. He saves me. And I sing songs of praise about him.
—*Isaiah 12:2 (ERV)*

I know the LORD is always with me. I will not be shaken, for he is right beside me.
—*Psalm 16:8 (NLT)*

I will refresh the weary and satisfy the faint.

—*Jeremiah 31:25 (NIV)*

Behold, I will bring it health and healing; I will heal them and reveal to them the abundance of peace and truth.

—*Jeremiah 33:6 (NKJV)*

Confess your sins to each other and pray for each other so that you may be healed. The earnest prayer of a righteous person has great power and produces wonderful results.

—*James 5:16 (NLT)*

O LORD my God, I cried out to You, and You healed me.

—Psalm 30:2 (NKJV)

Now may the God of peace who brought up our Lord Jesus from the dead, that great Shepherd of the sheep, through the blood of the everlasting covenant, make you complete in every good work to do His will, working in you what is well pleasing in His sight, through Jesus Christ, to whom be glory forever and ever. Amen.

—Hebrews 13:20–21 (NKJV)

Lord, if you heal me, I truly will be healed. Save me, and I truly will be saved. Lord, I praise you!

—Jeremiah 17:14 (ERV)

At that time, Hezekiah became sick and almost died. The prophet Isaiah son of Amoz went to Hezekiah. Isaiah said to Hezekiah, "The Lord says, 'Put your house in order, because you will die. You will not live!'" . . . Before Isaiah had left the middle courtyard, the word of the Lord came to him. The Lord said, "Go back and speak to Hezekiah, the leader of my people. Tell him, 'The Lord, the God of your ancestor David says: I have heard your prayer and I have seen your tears. So I will heal you. On the third day, you will go up to the temple of the Lord. And I will add 15 years to your life. I will save you and this city from the power of the king of Assyria. I will protect this city. I will do this for myself and because of the promise I made to my servant David.'"

—*2 Kings 20:1, 4–6 (ERV)*

When Israel was a child, I loved him,
and I called my son out of Egypt. . . .
I myself taught Israel how to walk,
leading him along by the hand. But he
doesn't know or even care that it was I
who took care of him. I led Israel along
with my ropes of kindness and love.
I lifted the yoke from his neck, and I
myself stooped to feed him.
        —*Hosea 11:1, 3–4 (NLT)*

Healing

THE HEART AND SPIRIT

*For God so loved the world that he
gave his one and only Son, that
whoever believes in him shall not
perish but have eternal life.*

—John 3:16 (NIV)

A Gentile woman who lived there came to him, pleading, "Have mercy on me, O Lord, Son of David! For my daughter is possessed by a demon that torments her severely." . . . "Dear woman," Jesus said to her, "your faith is great. Your request is granted." And her daughter was instantly healed.

—*Matthew 15:22, 28 (NLT)*

The Spirit of the LORD is upon me, for he has anointed me to bring Good News to the poor. He has sent me to proclaim that captives will be released, that the blind will see, that the oppressed will be set free.

—*Luke 4:18, quoting Isaiah 61:1*
(NLT)

On the third day a wedding took place at Cana in Galilee. Jesus' mother was there, and Jesus and his disciples had also been invited to the wedding.

—*John 2:1–2 (NIV)*

But if we confess (admit) our sins, then God will forgive our sins. We can trust God to do this. God does what is right. God will make us clean from all the wrong things we have done.

—*1 John 1:9 (ERV)*

At evening, when the sun had set, they brought to Him all who were sick and those who were demon-possessed. And the whole city was gathered together at the door.

—*Mark 1:32–33 (NKJV)*

Now all of us can come to the Father through the same Holy Spirit because of what Christ has done for us.

—*Ephesians 2:18 (NLT)*

So He got into a boat, crossed over, and came to His own city. Then behold, they brought to Him a paralytic lying on a bed. When Jesus saw their faith, He said to the paralytic, "Son, be of good cheer; your sins are forgiven you. . . . But that you may know that the Son of Man has power on earth to forgive sins"—then He said to the paralytic, "Arise, take up your bed, and go to your house." And he arose and departed to his house.

—*Matthew 9:1–2, 6–7 (NKJV)*

And God's peace will keep your hearts and minds in Christ Jesus. That peace which God gives is so great that we cannot understand it.

—*Philippians 4:7 (ERV)*

When the two men were leaving, some people brought another man to Jesus. This man could not talk because he had a demon inside him. Jesus forced the demon to leave the man. Then the man that couldn't talk was able to speak. The people were amazed and said, "We have never seen anything like this in Israel."

—*Matthew 9:32–33 (ERV)*

For Christ also suffered once for sins, the just for the unjust, that He might bring us to God, being put to death in the flesh but made alive by the Spirit.

—*1 Peter 3:18 (NKJV)*

He himself bore our sins in his body on the tree, so that we might die to sins and live for righteousness; by his wounds you have been healed.

—*1 Peter 2:24 (NIV)*

Therefore, brothers, since we have confidence to enter the Most Holy Place by the blood of Jesus . . . let us draw near to God with a sincere heart in full assurance of faith, having our hearts sprinkled to cleanse us from a guilty conscience and having our bodies washed with pure water. Let us hold unswervingly to the hope we profess, for he who promised is faithful.

—Hebrews 10:19, 22–23 (NIV)

For God loved the world so much that he gave his one and only Son, so that everyone who believes in him will not perish but have eternal life. God sent his Son into the world not to judge the world, but to save the world through him.

—John 3:16–17 (NLT)

Suddenly a man from the multitude cried out, saying, "Teacher, I implore You, look on my son, for he is my only child. And behold, a spirit seizes him, and he suddenly cries out; it convulses him so that he foams at the mouth, and it departs from him with great difficulty, bruising him." . . .

And as he was still coming, the demon threw [the child] down and convulsed him. Then Jesus rebuked the unclean spirit, healed the child, and gave him back to his father.

—*Luke 9:38–39, 42 (NKJV)*

Trust in the LORD with all your heart, and lean not on your own understanding; in all your ways acknowledge Him, and He shall direct your paths.

—*Proverbs 3:5–6 (NKJV)*

"Then I will sprinkle pure water on you and make you pure. I will wash away all your filth. I will wash away the filth from those nasty idols and make you pure." God said, "I will also put a new spirit in you and change your way of thinking. I will take out the heart of stone from your body and give you a tender, human heart. And I will put my Spirit inside you. I will change you so you will obey my laws. You will carefully obey my commands."

—*Ezekiel 36:25–27 (ERV)*

Since you have been raised to new life with Christ, set your sights on the realities of heaven, where Christ sits in the place of honor at God's right hand.

—*Colossians 3:1 (NLT)*

When Jesus saw their faith, he said to the paralytic, "Son, your sins are forgiven."

—*Mark 2:5 (NIV)*

# Healing THE HEART

The LORD is near to those who have a broken heart, and saves such as have a contrite spirit.

—*Psalm 34:18 (NKJV)*

If a person has peace in his mind, then his body will be healthy. But jealousy causes sickness in his body.

—*Proverbs 14:30 (ERV)*

He heals the brokenhearted and binds up their wounds.

—*Psalm 147:3 (NIV)*

Peace I leave with you, My peace I give to you; not as the world gives do I give to you. Let not your heart be troubled, neither let it be afraid.

—*John 14:27 (NKJV)*

For the Lord is the Spirit, and wherever the Spirit of the Lord is, there is freedom.

—*2 Corinthians 3:17 (NLT)*

Worry can take away a person's happiness. But a kind word can make a person happy.

—*Proverbs 12:25 (ERV)*

The light of the eyes rejoices the heart, and a good report makes the bones healthy.

—*Proverbs 15:30 (NKJV)*

You turned my wailing into dancing; you removed my sackcloth and clothed me with joy, that my heart may sing to you and not be silent. O LORD my God, I will give you thanks forever.

—*Psalm 30:11–12 (NIV)*

Blessed are you who hunger now, for you will be satisfied. Blessed are you who weep now, for you will laugh.

—*Luke 6:21 (NIV)*

I went to God for help. And he listened. He saved me from all the things I fear.

—*Psalm 34:4 (ERV)*

A cheerful heart is good medicine, but a broken spirit saps a person's strength.

—*Proverbs 17:22 (NLT)*

Happy is the man who is always reverent, but he who hardens his heart will fall into calamity.

—*Proverbs 28:14 (NKJV)*

Then shall the virgin rejoice in the dance, and the young men and the old, together; for I will turn their mourning to joy, will comfort them, and make them rejoice rather than sorrow.

—*Jeremiah 31:13 (NKJV)*

The Lord's servant says, "The Lord my Master put his Spirit in me. God chose me to tell good news to poor people and to comfort sad people. God sent me to tell the captives that they are free and to tell the prisoners that they have been set free."

—*Isaiah 61:1 (ERV)*

The fruit of righteousness will be peace; the effect of righteousness will be quietness and confidence forever.

—*Isaiah 32:17 (NIV)*

"Come now, let's settle this," says
the LORD. "Though your sins are like
scarlet, I will make them as white
as snow. Though they are red like
crimson, I will make them as white as
wool."
—*Isaiah 1:18 (NLT)*

I, I am the One who wipes away all your
sins. I do this to please myself. I will
not remember your sins.
—*Isaiah 43:25 (ERV)*

Then Peter said to them, "Repent, and
let every one of you be baptized in the
name of Jesus Christ for the remission
of sins; and you shall receive the gift of
the Holy Spirit."
—*Acts 2:38 (NKJV)*

All you thirsty people, Come drink water! Don't worry if you do not have money. Come, eat and drink until you are full! You do not need money; eat and drink until you are full. The food and wine cost nothing! Why waste your money on something that is not real food? Why should you work for something that does not really satisfy you? Listen very closely to me, and you will eat the good food. You will enjoy the food that satisfies your soul.

—*Isaiah 55:1–2 (ERV)*

Through this man Jesus there is forgiveness for your sins. Everyone who believes in him is declared right with God—something the law of Moses could never do.

—*Acts 13:38–39 (NLT)*

I will heal their waywardness and love them freely, for my anger has turned away from them.

—*Hosea 14:4 (NIV)*

If you openly say, "Jesus is Lord," and if you believe in your heart that God raised Jesus from death, then you will be saved.

—*Romans 10:9 (ERV)*

Jesus answered, "Everyone who drinks this water will be thirsty again, but whoever drinks the water I give him will never thirst. Indeed, the water I give him will become in him a spring of water welling up to eternal life."

—*John 4:13–14 (NIV)*

Yes, this anguish was good for me, for you have rescued me from death and forgiven all my sins.

—*Isaiah 38:17 (NLT)*

Jesus spoke to the people once more and said, "I am the light of the world. If you follow me, you won't have to walk in darkness, because you will have the light that leads to life."

—*John 8:12 (NLT)*

If my people who are called by my name become humble and pray, and look for me, and turn away from their evil ways, then I will hear them from heaven. And I will forgive their sin and I will heal their land.

—*2 Chronicles 7:14 (ERV)*

I will cleanse them from all their iniquity by which they have sinned against Me, and I will pardon all their iniquities by which they have sinned and by which they have transgressed against Me.

—*Jeremiah 33:8 (NKJV)*

Seek the LORD while He may be found, call upon Him while He is near. Let the wicked forsake his way, and the unrighteous man his thoughts; let him return to the LORD, and He will have mercy on him; and to our God, for He will abundantly pardon.

—*Isaiah 55:6–7 (NKJV)*

But look, the Lord my Master helps me. So no person can show me to be evil. All those people will become like worthless old clothes. Moths will eat them.

—*Isaiah 50:9 (ERV)*

But I call to God, and the LORD saves me. Evening, morning and noon I cry out in distress, and he hears my voice. He ransoms me unharmed from the battle waged against me, even though many oppose me.

—*Psalm 55:16–18 (NIV)*

I have swept away your offenses like a cloud, your sins like the morning mist. Return to me, for I have redeemed you.
    —*Isaiah 44:22 (NIV)*

[He] Himself bore our sins in His own body on the tree, that we, having died to sins, might live for righteousness—by whose stripes you were healed.
    —*1 Peter 2:24 (NKJV)*

Finding INNER STRENGTH

God is my strong fortress, and he makes my way perfect. He makes me as surefooted as a deer, enabling me to stand on mountain heights.

—*2 Samuel 22:33–34 (NLT)*

The LORD is my rock, my fortress and my deliverer; my God is my rock, in whom I take refuge. He is my shield and the horn of my salvation, my stronghold.

—*Psalm 18:2 (NIV)*

Don't worry, I am with you. Don't be afraid, I am your God. I will make you strong. I will help you. I will support you with my good right hand.

—*Isaiah 41:10 (ERV)*

Search for the LORD and for his strength; continually seek him.

—*1 Chronicles 16:11 (NLT)*

The LORD upholds all those who fall and lifts up all who are bowed down.

—*Psalm 145:14 (NIV)*

But blessed is the man who trusts in the LORD, whose confidence is in him. He will be like a tree planted by the water that sends out its roots by the stream. It does not fear when heat comes; its leaves are always green. It has no worries in a year of drought and never fails to bear fruit.

—*Jeremiah 17:7–8 (NIV)*

Wait on the LORD; be of good courage, and He shall strengthen your heart; wait, I say, on the LORD!

—*Psalm 27:14 (NKJV)*

I will search for my lost ones who strayed away, and I will bring them safely home again. I will bandage the injured and strengthen the weak. But I will destroy those who are fat and powerful. I will feed them, yes—feed them justice!

—*Ezekiel 34:16 (NLT)*

Surely you have heard and know that the Lord God is very wise. People can't learn everything he knows. The Lord does not become tired and need to rest. The Lord made all the faraway places on earth. The Lord lives forever. The Lord helps weak people to be strong. He causes the people without power to become powerful.

—*Isaiah 40:28–29 (ERV)*

The LORD is my shepherd, I shall not be in want. He makes me lie down in green pastures, he leads me beside quiet waters, he restores my soul. He guides me in paths of righteousness for his name's sake. Even though I walk through the valley of the shadow of death, I will fear no evil, for you are with me; your rod and your staff, they comfort me. You prepare a table before me in the presence of my enemies. You anoint my head with oil; my cup overflows. Surely goodness and love will follow me all the days of my life, and I will dwell in the house of the LORD forever.

—Psalm 23 (NIV)

The LORD gives his people strength. The LORD blesses them with peace.

—Psalm 29:11 (NLT)

Now David was greatly distressed,
for the people spoke of stoning him,
because the soul of all the people was
grieved, every man for his sons and
his daughters. But David strengthened
himself in the LORD his God.
—*1 Samuel 30:6 (NKJV)*

The LORD is my strength and my song;
he has become my salvation. He is my
God, and I will praise him, my father's
God, and I will exalt him.
—*Exodus 15:2 (NIV)*

For the eyes of the LORD run to and fro
throughout the whole earth, to show
Himself strong on behalf of those whose
heart is loyal to Him.
—*2 Chronicles 16:9 (NKJV)*

I am sad and tired. Give the command
and make me strong again.
—*Psalm 119:28 (ERV)*

For this reason, God, all your followers should pray to you. Your followers should pray even when troubles come like a great flood.

—*Psalm 32:6 (ERV)*

But I will sing of your strength, in the morning I will sing of your love; for you are my fortress, my refuge in times of trouble.

—*Psalm 59:16 (NIV)*

Gaining INNER PEACE

Peace I leave with you, My peace I give to you; not as the world gives do I give to you. Let not your heart be troubled, neither let it be afraid.

—*John 14:27 (NKJV)*

Don't worry about anything; instead, pray about everything. Tell God what you need, and thank him for all he has done. Then you will experience God's peace, which exceeds anything we can understand. His peace will guard your hearts and minds as you live in Christ Jesus.

—*Philippians 4:6–7 (NLT)*

For God is not a God of disorder but of peace, as in all the meetings of God's holy people.

> —*1 Corinthians 14:33 (NLT)*

People who love your teachings will find true peace. Nothing can make those people fall.

> —*Psalm 119:165 (ERV)*

And let the peace of God rule in your hearts, to which also you were called in one body; and be thankful.

> —*Colossians 3:15 (NKJV)*

Now may the Lord of peace himself give you peace at all times and in every way. The Lord be with all of you.

> —*2 Thessalonians 3:16 (NIV)*

But the fruit of the Spirit is love, joy, peace, longsuffering, kindness, goodness, faithfulness, gentleness, self-control. Against such there is no law.

> —*Galatians 5:22–23 (NKJV)*

Lord, you give true peace to people who depend on you, to people who trust you.

—*Isaiah 26:3 (ERV)*

Therefore, since we have been made right in God's sight by faith, we have peace with God because of what Jesus Christ our Lord has done for us.

—*Romans 5:1 (NLT)*

The LORD will give strength to His people; the LORD will bless His people with peace.

—*Psalm 29:11 (NKJV)*

But the wisdom that comes from God is like this: First, it is pure. It is also peaceful, gentle, and easy to please. This wisdom is always ready to help people who have trouble and to do good things for other people. This wisdom is always fair and honest.

—*James 3:17 (ERV)*

I will listen to what God the LORD will say; he promises peace to his people, his saints—but let them not return to folly.

> —*Psalm 85:8 (NIV)*

To all who are in Rome, beloved of God, called to be saints: Grace to you and peace from God our Father and the Lord Jesus Christ.

> —*Romans 1:7 (NKJV)*

LORD, you will grant us peace; all we have accomplished is really from you.

> —*Isaiah 26:12 (NLT)*

The mind of sinful man is death, but the mind controlled by the Spirit is life and peace.

> —*Romans 8:6 (NIV)*

I know I was ready to fall, but the
Lord supported his follower. I was
very worried and upset. But Lord, you
comforted me and made me happy!
—*Psalm 94:18–19 (ERV)*

The Lord's laws are right. They make
people happy. The Lord's commands
are good. They show people the right
way to live.
—*Psalm 19:8 (ERV)*

For great is the LORD and most worthy
of praise; he is to be feared above all
gods. . . . Splendor and majesty are
before him; strength and joy in his
dwelling place.
—*1 Chronicles 16:25, 27 (NIV)*

The LORD is my strength and my shield; my heart trusted in Him, and I am helped; therefore my heart greatly rejoices, and with my song I will praise Him.

—*Psalm 28:7 (NKJV)*

You have made known to me the paths of life; you will fill me with joy in your presence.

—*Acts 2:28 (NIV)*

Ask, using my name, and you will receive, and you will have abundant joy.

—*John 16:24 (NLT)*

Then I will go to the altar of God, to God my exceeding joy; and on the harp I will praise You, O God, my God.

—*Psalm 43:4 (NKJV)*

And so, dear brothers and sisters, we can boldly enter heaven's Most Holy Place because of the blood of Jesus. . . . Let us go right into the presence of God with sincere hearts fully trusting him. For our guilty consciences have been sprinkled with Christ's blood to make us clean, and our bodies have been washed with pure water. Let us hold tightly without wavering to the hope we affirm, for God can be trusted to keep his promise.

—*Hebrews 10:19, 22–23 (NLT)*

A person that smiles makes other people happy. And good news makes people feel better.

—*Proverbs 15:30 (ERV)*

He sends you rain and good crops and gives you food and joyful hearts.

—*Acts 14:17 (NLT)*

Therefore, if anyone is in Christ, he is a new creation; old things have passed away; behold, all things have become new. . . . For He made Him who knew no sin to be sin for us, that we might become the righteousness of God in Him.

—*2 Corinthians 5:17, 21 (NKJV)*

Nevertheless, I will bring health and healing to it; I will heal my people and will let them enjoy abundant peace and security.

—*Jeremiah 33:6 (NIV)*

I pray that the God who gives hope will fill you with much joy and peace while you trust in him. Then you will have more and more hope, and it will flow out of you by the power of the Holy Spirit.

—*Romans 15:13 (ERV)*

He will yet fill your mouth with laughing, and your lips with rejoicing.
     —*Job 8:21 (NKJV)*

Let all the people of Jerusalem shout his praise with joy! For great is the Holy One of Israel who lives among you.
     —*Isaiah 12:6 (NLT)*

For the kingdom of God is not eating and drinking, but righteousness and peace and joy in the Holy Spirit.
     —*Romans 14:17 (NKJV)*

Praise be to the God and Father of our Lord Jesus Christ. In Christ, God has given us every spiritual blessing in heaven.
     —*Ephesians 1:3 (ERV)*

Many people say, "Who will show us better times?" Let your face smile on us, LORD. You have given me greater joy than those who have abundant harvests of grain and new wine.

—*Psalm 4:6–7 (NLT)*

 REST FOR YOUR SPIRIT

Those who hope in the LORD will renew
their strength. They will soar on wings
like eagles; they will run and not grow
weary, they will walk and not be faint.
　　　—*Isaiah 40:31 (NIV)*

Come to me all you people that are
tired and have heavy burdens. I will
give you rest. Accept my work and learn
from me. I am gentle and humble in
spirit. And you will find rest for your
souls. Yes, the work that I ask you to
accept is easy. The burden I give you to
carry is not heavy.
　　　—*Matthew 11:28–30 (ERV)*

Return to your rest, O my soul, for the
LORD has dealt bountifully with you.
　　　—*Psalm 116:7 (NKJV)*

For I hold you by your right hand—I, the LORD your God. And I say to you, "Don't be afraid. I am here to help you."
—*Isaiah 41:13 (NLT)*

The law of the LORD is perfect, reviving the soul. The statutes of the LORD are trustworthy, making wise the simple.
—*Psalm 19:7 (NIV)*

Then Jesus said, "I am the bread that gives life. The person that comes to me will never be hungry. The person that believes in me will never be thirsty."
—*John 6:35 (ERV)*

But you are not in the flesh but in the Spirit, if indeed the Spirit of God dwells in you. Now if anyone does not have the Spirit of Christ, he is not His.
—*Romans 8:9 (NKJV)*

I waited patiently for the LORD; he turned to me and heard my cry. He lifted me out of the slimy pit, out of the mud and mire; he set my feet on a rock and gave me a firm place to stand.

—*Psalm 40:1–2 (NIV)*

The last day of the festival came. It was the most important day. On that day Jesus stood and said with a loud voice, "If a person is thirsty, let him come to me and drink. If a person believes in me, rivers of living water will flow out from his heart. That is what the Scriptures say."

—*John 7:37–38 (ERV)*

I wait quietly before God, for my victory comes from him. He alone is my rock and my salvation, my fortress where I will never be shaken.

—*Psalm 62:1–2 (NLT)*

A happy heart makes the face cheerful, but heartache crushes the spirit.

—*Proverbs 15:13 (NIV)*

Strengthen the weak hands, and make firm the feeble knees. Say to those who are fearful-hearted, "Be strong, do not fear! Behold, your God will come with vengeance, with the recompense of God; He will come and save you."

—*Isaiah 35:3–4 (NKJV)*

So don't remember the things that happened in the beginning. Don't think about the things that happened a long time ago. Why? Because I will do new things! Now you will grow like a new plant. Surely you know this is true. I really will make a road in the desert. I really will make rivers in the dry land.

—*Isaiah 43:18–19 (ERV)*

Hope deferred makes the heart sick,
but a dream fulfilled is a tree of life.
—*Proverbs 13:12 (NLT)*

The LORD is my shepherd; I shall not
want. He makes me to lie down in green
pastures; He leads me beside the still
waters. He restores my soul; He leads
me in the paths of righteousness for His
name's sake.
—*Psalm 23:1–3 (NKJV)*

And I will ask the Father, and he will
give you another Counselor to be with
you forever—the Spirit of truth. The
world cannot accept him, because it
neither sees him nor knows him. But
you know him, for he lives with you and
will be in you.
—*John 14:16–17 (NIV)*

Find rest, O my soul, in God alone; my
hope comes from him.
—*Psalm 62:5 (NIV)*

So, trust the Lord always. Why? Because in the Lord YAH, you have a place of safety forever!
—*Isaiah 26:4 (ERV)*

And because you are sons, God has sent forth the Spirit of His Son into your hearts, crying out, "Abba, Father!"
—*Galatians 4:6 (NKJV)*

Prayers FOR HEALING THE HEART

My good God, answer me when I pray
to you! Hear my prayer and be kind to
me! Give me some relief from all my
troubles!
>   —*Psalm 4:1 (ERV)*

Turn to me and have mercy, for I
am alone and in deep distress. My
problems go from bad to worse. Oh,
save me from them all! Feel my pain
and see my trouble. Forgive all my sins.
>   —*Psalm 25:16–18 (NLT)*

Look upon my suffering and rescue
me, for I have not forgotten your
instructions.
>   —*Psalm 119:153 (NLT)*

Save me, O God! For the waters have come up to my neck. I sink in deep mire, where there is no standing; I have come into deep waters, where the floods overflow me.

—*Psalm 69:1–2 (NKJV)*

My soul is weary with sorrow; strengthen me according to your word.

—*Psalm 119:28 (NIV)*

I pray that God will open your minds to see his truth. Then you will know the hope that God has chosen us to have. You will know that the blessings God has promised his holy people are rich and glorious.

—*Ephesians 1:18 (ERV)*

I would comfort myself in sorrow; my heart is faint in me.

—*Jeremiah 8:18 (NKJV)*

I know that my Redeemer lives, and
that in the end he will stand upon
the earth. And after my skin has been
destroyed, yet in my flesh I will see
God; I myself will see him with my own
eyes—I, and not another. How my heart
yearns within me!
 —*Job 19:25–27 (NIV)*

From the ends of the earth, I cry to you
for help when my heart is overwhelmed.
Lead me to the towering rock of safety,
for you are my safe refuge, a fortress
where my enemies cannot reach me.
 —*Psalm 61:2–3 (NLT)*

May your eyes be open to your
servant's plea and to the plea of your
people Israel, and may you listen to
them whenever they cry out to you.
 —*1 Kings 8:52 (NIV)*

Prayers FOR SPIRITUAL HEALING

As the deer pants for streams of water, so my soul pants for you, O God. My soul thirsts for God, for the living God. When can I go and meet with God?
—*Psalm 42:1–2 (NIV)*

"O Lord," I prayed, "have mercy on me. Heal me, for I have sinned against you."
—*Psalm 41:4 (NLT)*

God, be merciful to me, because of your great loving kindness, because of your great mercy, erase all my sins. God, scrub away my guilt. Wash away my sins, make me clean again!
—*Psalm 51:1–2 (ERV)*

God, create a pure heart in me! Make my spirit strong again!
—*Psalm 51:10 (ERV)*

O Israel, return to the LORD your God, for you have stumbled because of your iniquity; take words with you, and return to the LORD. Say to Him, "Take away all iniquity; receive us graciously, for we will offer the sacrifices of our lips."

—*Hosea 14:1–2 (NKJV)*

Into Your hand I commit my spirit; You have redeemed me, O LORD God of truth.

—*Psalm 31:5 (NKJV)*

So Moses went back to the LORD and said, "Oh, what a great sin these people have committed! They have made themselves gods of gold. But now, please forgive their sin—but if not, then blot me out of the book you have written."

—*Exodus 32:31–32 (NIV)*

Do not be angry beyond measure,
O LORD; do not remember our sins
forever. Oh, look upon us, we pray, for
we are all your people.

     —Isaiah 64:9 (NIV)

Healing

THE BODY AND MIND

And do not be conformed to this world, but be transformed by the renewing of your mind, that you may prove what is that good and acceptable and perfect will of God.

—Romans 12:2 (NKJV)

Jesus HEALED THE MIND AND BODY

As the sun went down that evening, people throughout the village brought sick family members to Jesus. No matter what their diseases were, the touch of his hand healed every one.
—*Luke 4:40 (NLT)*

The people were really amazed. The people said, "Jesus does everything in a good way. Jesus makes deaf people able to hear. And people that can't talk— Jesus makes them able to talk."
—*Mark 7:37 (ERV)*

Then one was brought to Him who was demon-possessed, blind and mute; and He healed him, so that the blind and mute man both spoke and saw.
—*Matthew 12:22 (NKJV)*

When Jesus arrived at Peter's house, Peter's mother-in-law was sick in bed with a high fever. But when Jesus touched her hand, the fever left her. Then she got up and prepared a meal for him.

—*Matthew 8:14–15 (NLT)*

Jesus left that place and went into their synagogue. In the synagogue there was a man with a crippled hand. Some Jews there were looking for a reason to accuse Jesus of doing wrong. So they asked Jesus, "Is it right to heal on the Sabbath day?" . . . Then Jesus said to the man with the crippled hand, "Let me see your hand." The man put his hand out for Jesus, and the hand became well again, the same as the other hand.

—*Matthew 12:9–10, 13 (ERV)*

Soon afterward, Jesus went to a town called Nain, and his disciples and a large crowd went along with him. As he approached the town gate, a dead person was being carried out—the only son of his mother, and she was a widow. And a large crowd from the town was with her. When the Lord saw her, his heart went out to her and he said, "Don't cry."

Then he went up and touched the coffin, and those carrying it stood still. He said, "Young man, I say to you, get up!" The dead man sat up and began to talk, and Jesus gave him back to his mother.

—Luke 7:11–15 (NIV)

After Jesus left the girl's home, two blind men followed along behind him, shouting, "Son of David, have mercy on us!"

They went right into the house where he was staying, and Jesus asked them, "Do you believe I can make you see?"

"Yes, Lord," they told him, "we do."

Then he touched their eyes and said, "Because of your faith, it will happen." Then their eyes were opened, and they could see! Jesus sternly warned them, "Don't tell anyone about this."

—*Matthew 9:27–30 (NLT)*

Then Jesus said, "Stand up! Pick up your bed and walk." Then immediately the man was well. The man picked up his bed and started walking. The day all this happened was a Sabbath day.

—*John 5:8–9 (ERV)*

Jesus returned to the Sea of Galilee and climbed a hill and sat down. A vast crowd brought to him people who were lame, blind, crippled, those who couldn't speak, and many others. They laid them before Jesus, and he healed them all. The crowd was amazed! Those who hadn't been able to speak were talking, the crippled were made well, the lame were walking, and the blind could see again! And they praised the God of Israel.

—*Matthew 15:29–31 (NLT)*

"And I will bring your health back. And I will heal your wounds." This message is from the Lord. "Why? Because other people said you were outcasts. Those people said, 'No one cares about Zion.'"

—*Jeremiah 30:17 (ERV)*

And suddenly, a woman who had a flow of blood for twelve years came from behind and touched the hem of His garment. For she said to herself, "If only I may touch His garment, I shall be made well." But Jesus turned around, and when He saw her He said, "Be of good cheer, daughter; your faith has made you well." And the woman was made well from that hour.

—*Matthew 9:20–22 (NKJV)*

As he was going into a village, ten men who had leprosy met him. They stood at a distance and called out in a loud voice, "Jesus, Master, have pity on us!"

When he saw them, he said, "Go, show yourselves to the priests." And as they went, they were cleansed.

—*Luke 17:12–14 (NIV)*

Jesus led him away from the crowd so they could be alone. He put his fingers into the man's ears. Then, spitting on his own fingers, he touched the man's tongue. Looking up to heaven, he sighed and said, "Ephphatha," which means, "Be opened!" Instantly the man could hear perfectly, and his tongue was freed so he could speak plainly!
—*Mark 7:33–35 (NLT)*

On a Sabbath Jesus was teaching in one of the synagogues, and a woman was there who had been crippled by a spirit for eighteen years. She was bent over and could not straighten up at all. When Jesus saw her, he called her forward and said to her, "Woman, you are set free from your infirmity." Then he put his hands on her, and immediately she straightened up and praised God.
—*Luke 13:10–13 (NIV)*

A man that had leprosy came to Jesus. The man bowed on his knees and begged Jesus, "You have the power to heal me if you want." Jesus felt sorry for the man. So Jesus touched the man and said, "I want to heal you. Be healed!" Immediately the leprosy disappeared, and he was healed.

          —*Mark 1:40–42 (ERV)*

Then Jesus said to the centurion, "Go! It will be done just as you believed it would." And his servant was healed at that very hour.

          —*Matthew 8:13 (NIV)*

People GOD USED TO HEAL OTHERS

Jesus was very surprised because those people did not have faith. Then Jesus went to other villages in that area and taught. Jesus called the twelve followers together. Jesus sent them out in groups of two. Jesus gave them power over evil spirits. . . . The followers left there and went to other places. They talked to the people and told them to change their hearts and lives. The followers forced many demons out of people. And the followers put olive oil on sick people and healed them.

—*Mark 6:6–7, 12–13 (ERV)*

Now it came to pass, as Peter went through all parts of the country, that he also came down to the saints who dwelt in Lydda. There he found a certain man named Aeneas, who had been bedridden eight years and was paralyzed. And Peter said to him, "Aeneas, Jesus the Christ heals you. Arise and make your bed." Then he arose immediately.

—*Acts 9:32–34 (NKJV)*

They devoted themselves to the apostles' teaching and to the fellowship, to the breaking of bread and to prayer. Everyone was filled with awe, and many wonders and miraculous signs were done by the apostles.

—*Acts 2:42–43 (NIV)*

Now it happened after these things that the son of the woman who owned the house became sick. And his sickness was so serious that there was no breath left in him. . . .

And [Elijah] said to her, "Give me your son." So he took him out of her arms and carried him to the upper room where he was staying, and laid him on his own bed. Then he cried out to the LORD and said, "O LORD my God, have You also brought tragedy on the widow with whom I lodge, by killing her son?" And he stretched himself out on the child three times, and cried out to the LORD and said, "O LORD my God, I pray, let this child's soul come back to him." Then the LORD heard the voice of Elijah; and the soul of the child came back to him, and he revived.

—*1 Kings 17:17, 19–22 (NKJV)*

While they were at Lystra, Paul and Barnabas came upon a man with crippled feet. He had been that way from birth, so he had never walked. He was sitting and listening as Paul preached. Looking straight at him, Paul realized he had faith to be healed. So Paul called to him in a loud voice, "Stand up!" And the man jumped to his feet and started walking.

—*Acts 14:8–10 (NLT)*

Philip, for example, went to the city of Samaria and told the people there about the Messiah. Crowds listened intently to Philip because they were eager to hear his message and see the miraculous signs he did. Many evil spirits were cast out, screaming as they left their victims. And many who had been paralyzed or lame were healed. So there was great joy in that city.

—*Acts 8:5–8 (NLT)*

When they were going into the temple yard, a man was there. This man had been crippled all his life. He could not walk, so some friends carried him. His friends brought him to the temple every day. They put the crippled man by one of the gates outside the temple. It was called Beautiful Gate. There the man begged for money from the people going to the temple. . . . That day the man saw Peter and John going into the temple yard. He asked them for money. Then Peter held the man's right hand and lifted him up. Immediately the man's feet and legs became strong. The man jumped up, stood on his feet, and began to walk. He went into the temple yard with them. The man was walking and jumping, and he was praising God.

—Acts 3:2–3, 7–8 (ERV)

At Joppa there was a certain disciple named Tabitha, which is translated Dorcas. This woman was full of good works and charitable deeds which she did. But it happened in those days that she became sick and died. When they had washed her, they laid her in an upper room. . . . But Peter put them all out, and knelt down and prayed. And turning to the body he said, "Tabitha, arise." And she opened her eyes, and when she saw Peter she sat up. Then he gave her his hand and lifted her up; and when he had called the saints and widows, he presented her alive.

—*Acts 9:36–37, 40–41 (NKJV)*

And Ananias went his way and entered the house; and laying his hands on him he said, "Brother Saul, the Lord Jesus, who appeared to you on the road as you came, has sent me that you may receive your sight and be filled with the Holy Spirit." Immediately there fell from his eyes something like scales, and he received his sight at once; and he arose and was baptized.

—*Acts 9:17–18 (NKJV)*

 *Healing* THE MIND

Search me, O God, and know my heart; test me and know my anxious thoughts. Point out anything in me that offends you, and lead me along the path of everlasting life.

—*Psalm 139:23–24 (NLT)*

Let the wicked change their ways and banish the very thought of doing wrong. Let them turn to the LORD that he may have mercy on them. Yes, turn to our God, for he will forgive generously.

—*Isaiah 55:7 (NLT)*

Jesus replied: "Love the Lord your God with all your heart and with all your soul and with all your mind."

—*Matthew 22:37 (NIV)*

And do not be conformed to this world, but be transformed by the renewing of your mind, that you may prove what is that good and acceptable and perfect will of God.

—*Romans 12:2 (NKJV)*

Do not be anxious about anything, but in everything, by prayer and petition, with thanksgiving, present your requests to God. And the peace of God, which transcends all understanding, will guard your hearts and your minds in Christ Jesus.

Finally, brothers, whatever is true, whatever is noble, whatever is right, whatever is pure, whatever is lovely, whatever is admirable—if anything is excellent or praiseworthy—think about such things.

—*Philippians 4:6–8 (NIV)*

Nothing in all creation is hidden from God's sight. Everything is uncovered and laid bare before the eyes of him to whom we must give account.

Therefore, since we have a great high priest who has gone through the heavens, Jesus the Son of God, let us hold firmly to the faith we profess. For we do not have a high priest who is unable to sympathize with our weaknesses, but we have one who has been tempted in every way, just as we are—yet was without sin. Let us then approach the throne of grace with confidence, so that we may receive mercy and find grace to help us in our time of need.

—*Hebrews 4:13–16 (NIV)*

Lord, you give true peace to people who depend on you, to people who trust you.

—*Isaiah 26:3 (ERV)*

The mind of sinful man is death, but the mind controlled by the Spirit is life and peace.

—Romans 8:6 (NIV)

Are any of you suffering hardships? You should pray. Are any of you happy? You should sing praises. Are any of you sick? You should call for the elders of the church to come and pray over you, anointing you with oil in the name of the Lord. Such a prayer offered in faith will heal the sick, and the Lord will make you well. And if you have committed any sins, you will be forgiven.

Confess your sins to each other and pray for each other so that you may be healed. The earnest prayer of a righteous person has great power and produces wonderful results.

—*James 5:13–16 (NLT)*

Now you are the body of Christ, and each one of you is a part of it. And in the church God has appointed first of all apostles, second prophets, third teachers, then workers of miracles, also those having gifts of healing, those able to help others, those with gifts of administration, and those speaking in different kinds of tongues.

—*1 Corinthians 12:27–28 (NIV)*

Persistence IN PRAYER

Also, the Spirit helps us. We are very weak, but the Spirit helps us with our weakness. We don't know how to pray like we should. But the Spirit himself speaks to God for us. The Spirit begs God for us. The Spirit speaks to God with deep feelings that words cannot explain.

> —*Romans 8:26 (ERV)*

Rejoice in our confident hope. Be patient in trouble, and keep on praying.

> —*Romans 12:12 (NLT)*

One day soon afterward Jesus went up on a mountain to pray, and he prayed to God all night.

> —*Luke 6:12 (NLT)*

That is why we always pray for you. We ask our God to help you live the good way that he called you to live. The goodness you have makes you want to do good. And the faith you have makes you work. We pray that with his power God will help you do these things more and more. We pray all this so that the name of our Lord Jesus Christ can have glory in you. And you can have glory in him. That glory comes from the grace (kindness) of our God and the Lord Jesus Christ.

—*2 Thessalonians 1:11–12 (ERV)*

Now she who is really a widow, and left alone, trusts in God and continues in supplications and prayers night and day.

—*1 Timothy 5:5 (NKJV)*

One day Jesus told his disciples a story to show that they should always pray and never give up. "There was a judge in a certain city," he said, "who neither feared God nor cared about people. A widow of that city came to him repeatedly, saying, 'Give me justice in this dispute with my enemy.' The judge ignored her for a while, but finally he said to himself, 'I don't fear God or care about people, but this woman is driving me crazy. I'm going to see that she gets justice, because she is wearing me out with her constant requests!'"

—*Luke 18:1–5 (NLT)*

Pray in the Spirit at all times. Pray with all kinds of prayers, and ask for everything you need. To do this you must always be ready. Never give up. Always pray for all God's people.

—*Ephesians 6:18 (ERV)*

Continue earnestly in prayer, being vigilant in it with thanksgiving.
—*Colossians 4:2 (NKJV)*

Pray continually.
—*1 Thessalonians 5:17 (NIV)*

I tell you the truth. You can say to this mountain, "Go, mountain, fall into the sea." And if you have no doubts in your mind and believe that the thing you say will happen, then God will do it for you. So I tell you to ask for things in prayer. And if you believe that you have received those things, then they will be yours. When you are praying, and you remember that you are angry with another person about something, then forgive that person. Forgive them so that your Father in heaven will also forgive your sins.
—*Mark 11:23–25 (ERV)*

Lord, I have many troubles. So be kind to me. I am so upset that my eyes are hurting. My throat and stomach are aching. My life is ending in sadness. My years are passing away in sighing. My troubles are taking away my strength. My strength is leaving me. . . . Lord, I trust you. You are my God. My life is in your hands. Save me from my enemies. Some people are chasing me. Save me from them.

    —Psalm 31:9–10, 14–15 (ERV)

Heal me, O LORD, and I will be healed; save me and I will be saved, for you are the one I praise.

    —Jeremiah 17:14 (NIV)

Return, O LORD, and rescue me. Save me because of your unfailing love.
—*Psalm 6:4 (NLT)*

Lord, don't leave me! You are my strength. Hurry and help me!
—*Psalm 22:19 (ERV)*

Do not abandon me, O LORD. Do not stand at a distance, my God. Come quickly to help me, O Lord my savior.
—*Psalm 38:21–22 (NLT)*

Beloved, I pray that you may prosper in all things and be in health, just as your soul prospers.
—*3 John 2 (NKJV)*

Responses TO HEALING

As Jesus was getting into the boat, the
man who had been demon possessed
begged to go with him. But Jesus said,
"No, go home to your family, and tell
them everything the Lord has done for
you and how merciful he has been."
So the man started off to visit the Ten
Towns of that region and began to
proclaim the great things Jesus had
done for him; and everyone was amazed
at what he told them.

> —Mark 5:18–20 (NLT)

He jumped up, stood on his feet, and
began to walk! Then, walking, leaping,
and praising God, he went into the
Temple with them.

> —Acts 3:8 (NLT)

But Peter put them all out, and knelt down and prayed. And turning to the body he said, "Tabitha, arise." And she opened her eyes, and when she saw Peter she sat up. Then he gave her his hand and lifted her up; and when he had called the saints and widows, he presented her alive. And it became known throughout all Joppa, and many believed on the Lord.

—*Acts 9:40–42 (NKJV)*

Then he went up and touched the coffin, and those carrying it stood still. He said, "Young man, I say to you, get up!" The dead man sat up and began to talk, and Jesus gave him back to his mother. They were all filled with awe and praised God. "A great prophet has appeared among us," they said. "God has come to help his people."

—*Luke 7:14–16 (NIV)*

Jesus traveled throughout the region of Galilee, teaching in the synagogues and announcing the Good News about the Kingdom. And he healed every kind of disease and illness. News about him spread as far as Syria, and people soon began bringing to him all who were sick. And whatever their sickness or disease, or if they were demon-possessed or epileptic or paralyzed—he healed them all. Large crowds followed him wherever he went—people from Galilee, the Ten Towns, Jerusalem, from all over Judea, and from east of the Jordan River.

—*Matthew 4:23–25 (NLT)*

Bless the LORD, O my soul, and forget not all His benefits: Who forgives all your iniquities, Who heals all your diseases,

—*Psalm 103:2–3 (NKJV)*

"The Son of Man has power on earth to forgive sins. But how can I prove this to you? Maybe you are thinking it was easy for me to say, 'Your sins are forgiven.' No one could see if it really happened. But what if I say to the man, 'Stand up and walk'? Then you will be able to see that I really have this power." So Jesus said to the paralyzed man, "Stand up. Take your mat and go home." And the man stood up and went home. The people saw this and they were amazed. The people praised God for giving power like this to people.

—*Matthew 9:6–8 (ERV)*

And lest I should be exalted above measure by the abundance of the revelations, a thorn in the flesh was given to me, a messenger of Satan to buffet me, lest I be exalted above measure. Concerning this thing I pleaded with the Lord three times that it might depart from me. And He said to me, "My grace is sufficient for you, for My strength is made perfect in weakness." Therefore most gladly I will rather boast in my infirmities, that the power of Christ may rest upon me. Therefore I take pleasure in infirmities, in reproaches, in needs, in persecutions, in distresses, for Christ's sake. For when I am weak, then I am strong.

—2 Corinthians 12:7–10 (NKJV)

One of the men in the crowd spoke up and said, "Teacher, I brought my son so you could heal him. He is possessed by an evil spirit that won't let him talk. And whenever this spirit seizes him, it throws him violently to the ground. Then he foams at the mouth and grinds his teeth and becomes rigid. So I asked your disciples to cast out the evil spirit, but they couldn't do it." . . .

So they brought the boy. But when the evil spirit saw Jesus, it threw the child into a violent convulsion, and he fell to the ground, writhing and foaming at the mouth.

"How long has this been happening?" Jesus asked the boy's father.

He replied, "Since he was a little boy. The spirit often throws him into the fire or into water, trying to kill him. Have mercy on us and help us, if you can."

"What do you mean, 'If I can'?" Jesus

asked. "Anything is possible if a person believes."

The father instantly cried out, "I do believe, but help me overcome my unbelief!"

—Mark 9:17–18, 20–24 (NLT)

Healing

BROKEN RELATIONSHIPS

Love is patient, love is kind. It does not envy, it does not boast, it is not proud. It is not rude, it is not self-seeking, it is not easily angered, it keeps no record of wrongs. Love does not delight in evil but rejoices with the truth. It always protects, always trusts, always hopes, always perseveres. Love never fails. But where there are prophecies, they will cease; where there are tongues, they will be stilled; where there is knowledge, it will pass away.

—1 Corinthians 13:4–8 (NIV)

Healing RELATIONSHIPS

He who covers over an offense promotes love, but whoever repeats the matter separates close friends.

—*Proverbs 17:9 (NIV)*

If a person speaks words without thinking, then those words can hurt like a sword. But a wise person is careful with the things he says. His words can heal those hurts.

—*Proverbs 12:18 (ERV)*

A gentle answer deflects anger, but harsh words make tempers flare.

—*Proverbs 15:1 (NLT)*

When a man's ways please the LORD, He makes even his enemies to be at peace with him.

—*Proverbs 16:7 (NKJV)*

A few days later, Paul said to Barnabas, "We told the message of the Lord in many towns. We should go back to all those towns to visit the brothers and sisters and see how they are doing." Barnabas wanted to bring John Mark with them too. But on their first trip John Mark had left them at Pamphylia; he did not continue with them in the work. So Paul did not think it was a good idea to take him. Paul and Barnabas had a big argument about this. They separated and went different ways. Barnabas sailed to Cyprus and took Mark with him. Paul chose Silas to go with him. The brothers in Antioch put Paul into the Lord's care and sent him out.

—*Acts 15:36–40 (ERV)*

Everyone wants a true and loyal
friend—it is better to be poor than a
person that can't be trusted.
—*Proverbs 19:22 (ERV)*

Gentle words are a tree of life; a
deceitful tongue crushes the spirit.
—*Proverbs 15:4 (NLT)*

Then Peter came to Jesus and asked,
"Lord, how many times shall I forgive
my brother when he sins against me?
Up to seven times?"

Jesus answered, "I tell you, not seven
times, but seventy-seven times."
—*Matthew 18:21–22 (NIV)*

My fellow prisoner Aristarchus sends
you his greetings, as does Mark, the
cousin of Barnabas. (You have received
instructions about him; if he comes to
you, welcome him.)
—*Colossians 4:10 (NIV)*

Yes, if you forgive other people for the things they do wrong, then your Father in heaven will also forgive you for the things you do wrong. But if you don't forgive the wrong things people do to you, then your Father in heaven will not forgive the wrong things you do.

—*Matthew 6:14–15 (ERV)*

Suppose a person is suing you, and you are going with him to court. You should try hard to settle it on the way. If you don't settle it, he may take you to the judge. And the judge will throw you into jail.

—*Luke 12:58 (ERV)*

What IS OUR RESPONSIBILITY?

Put on tender mercies, kindness, humility, meekness, longsuffering, bearing with one another, and forgiving one another, if anyone has a complaint against another; even as Christ forgave you, so you also must do. But above all these things put on love, which is the bond of perfection.

—Colossians 3:12–14 (NKJV)

See that no one renders evil for evil to anyone, but always pursue what is good both for yourselves and for all.

—1 Thessalonians 5:15 (NKJV)

When arguing with your neighbor, don't betray another person's secret.

—Proverbs 25:9 (NLT)

Therefore let us stop passing judgment on one another. Instead, make up your mind not to put any stumbling block or obstacle in your brother's way.
—*Romans 14:13 (NIV)*

Stay away from foolish and stupid arguments. You know that those arguments grow into bigger arguments.
—*2 Timothy 2:23 (ERV)*

But to you who are willing to listen, I say, love your enemies! Do good to those who hate you. Bless those who curse you. Pray for those who hurt you.
—*Luke 6:27–28 (NLT)*

Do not withhold good from those to whom it is due, when it is in the power of your hand to do so.
—*Proverbs 3:27 (NKJV)*

Therefore, if you are offering your gift at the altar and there remember that your brother has something against you, leave your gift there in front of the altar. First go and be reconciled to your brother; then come and offer your gift.

—Matthew 5:23–24 (NIV)

Never pay back evil with more evil. Do things in such a way that everyone can see you are honorable. Do all that you can to live in peace with everyone. Dear friends, never take revenge. Leave that to the righteous anger of God. For the Scriptures say, "I will take revenge; I will pay them back," says the LORD.

—Romans 12:17–19 (NLT)

Yes, if you forgive other people for the things they do wrong, then your Father in heaven will also forgive you for the things you do wrong. But if you don't forgive the wrong things people do to you, then your Father in heaven will not forgive the wrong things you do.
—*Matthew 6:14–15 (ERV)*

Do for other people what you want them to do for you.
　　—*Luke 6:31 (ERV)*

Let us therefore make every effort to do what leads to peace and to mutual edification.
　　—*Romans 14:19 (NIV)*

Since God chose you to be the holy people he loves, you must clothe yourselves with tenderhearted mercy, kindness, humility, gentleness, and patience.
　　—*Colossians 3:12 (NLT)*

Hate causes arguments. But love forgives every wrong thing people do.
　　—*Proverbs 10:12 (ERV)*

It is honorable for a man to stop striving, since any fool can start a quarrel.
—*Proverbs 20:3 (NKJV)*

"The most important one," answered Jesus, "is this: 'Hear, O Israel, the Lord our God, the Lord is one. Love the Lord your God with all your heart and with all your soul and with all your mind and with all your strength.' The second is this: 'Love your neighbor as yourself.' There is no commandment greater than these."
—*Mark 12:29–31 (NIV)*

Do everything in love.
—*1 Corinthians 16:14 (NIV)*

The father of a good person is very happy. If a person has a wise child, then that child brings joy.
—*Proverbs 23:24 (ERV)*

THE PATH TO

Wholeness

*The commandments of the
LORD are right, bringing joy
to the heart. The commands
of the LORD are clear, giving
insight for living.*

—Psalm 19:8 (NLT)

Wholeness
COMES THROUGH VIRTUE

A sound heart is life to the body, but envy is rottenness to the bones.
>   —*Proverbs 14:30 (NKJV)*

A person will be truly happy if he doesn't follow the advice of bad people and doesn't live like sinners and doesn't feel at home with people who don't respect God. A good person loves the Lord's teachings. He thinks about them day and night. So that person becomes strong like a tree planted by streams of water He is like a tree that makes fruit at the right time. He is like a tree with leaves that don't die. Everything he does is successful.
>   —*Psalm 1:1–3 (ERV)*

You will experience all these blessings if you obey the LORD your God: Your towns and your fields will be blessed. Your children and your crops will be blessed. The offspring of your herds and flocks will be blessed. Your fruit baskets and breadboards will be blessed. Wherever you go and whatever you do, you will be blessed.

—Deuteronomy 28:2–6 (NLT)

Rejoice always, pray without ceasing, in everything give thanks; for this is the will of God in Christ Jesus for you.

—1 Thessalonians 5:16–18 (NKJV)

My son, do not forget my teaching, but keep my commands in your heart, for they will prolong your life many years and bring you prosperity.

—Proverbs 3:1–2 (NIV)

The teachings of a wise person give life. Those words will help you in times of trouble.

   —Proverbs 13:14 (ERV)

Do not be wise in your own eyes; fear the LORD and depart from evil. It will be health to your flesh, and strength to your bones.

   —Proverbs 3:7–8 (NKJV)

The mind of sinful man is death, but the mind controlled by the Spirit is life and peace.

   —Romans 8:6 (NIV)

My child, pay attention to what I say. Listen carefully to my words. Don't lose sight of them. Let them penetrate deep into your heart, for they bring life to those who find them, and healing to their whole body.

   —Proverbs 4:20–22 (NLT)

"I will tell you the kind of special day I want—a day to make people free. I want a day that you take the burdens off people. I want a day when you make the troubled people free. I want a day when you take the burdens from their shoulders. I want you to share your food with the hungry people. I want you to find poor people that don't have homes, and I want you to bring them into your own homes. When you see a man that has no clothes—give him your clothes! Don't hide from helping those people; they are just like you." If you do these things, your light will begin shining like the light of dawn. Then your wounds will heal. Your "Goodness" (God) will walk in front of you, and the Glory of the Lord will come following behind you.

—*Isaiah 58:6–8 (ERV)*

Completeness IN CHRIST

And I am certain that God, who began the good work within you, will continue his work until it is finally finished on the day when Christ Jesus returns.

    —Philippians 1:6 (NLT)

The LORD redeems his servants; no one will be condemned who takes refuge in him.

    —Psalm 34:22 (NIV)

But, for my followers, goodness will shine on you like the rising sun. And it will bring healing power like the sun's rays. You will be free and happy, like calves freed from their stalls.

    —Malachi 4:2 (ERV)

All praise to God, the Father of our Lord Jesus Christ. It is by his great mercy that we have been born again, because God raised Jesus Christ from the dead. Now we live with great expectation.

—*1 Peter 1:3 (NLT)*

For the Lamb who is in the midst of the throne will shepherd them and lead them to living fountains of waters. And God will wipe away every tear from their eyes.

—*Revelation 7:17 (NKJV)*

The Spirit of God, who raised Jesus from the dead, lives in you. And just as God raised Christ Jesus from the dead, he will give life to your mortal bodies by this same Spirit living within you.

—*Romans 8:11 (NLT)*

Through Christ Jesus the law of the Spirit of life set me free from the law of sin and death.

—*Romans 8:2 (NIV)*

So you have sorrow now, but I will see you again; then you will rejoice, and no one can rob you of that joy. At that time you won't need to ask me for anything. I tell you the truth, you will ask the Father directly, and he will grant your request because you use my name.

—*John 16:22–23 (NLT)*

The Lord is my strength. He saves me, and I sing songs of praise to him. The Lord is my God, and I praise him. The Lord is the God of my ancestors, and I honor him.

—*Exodus 15:2 (ERV)*

For God so loved the world that He gave His only begotten Son, that whoever believes in Him should not perish but have everlasting life. For God did not send His Son into the world to condemn the world, but that the world through Him might be saved.
—*John 3:16–17 (NKJV)*

So surely the blood of Christ can do much, much more. Christ offered himself through the eternal Spirit as a perfect sacrifice to God. His blood will make us fully clean from the evil things we have done. His blood will make us pure even in our hearts. We are made pure so that we can worship (serve) the living God.
—*Hebrews 9:14 (ERV)*

For in this we groan, earnestly desiring to be clothed with our habitation which is from heaven.
—*2 Corinthians 5:2 (NKJV)*

Prayers OF PRAISE

The LORD lives! Blessed be my Rock!
Let God be exalted, the Rock of my
salvation!
> —2 Samuel 22:47 (NKJV)

I prayed and you helped me! You
changed my crying into dancing. You
took away my clothes of sadness. And
you wrapped me in happiness. Lord,
my God, I will praise you forever, so
there will never be silence, and there
will always be someone singing songs to
honor you.
> —Psalm 30:11–12 (ERV)

O LORD my God, I cried out to You, and
You healed me.
> —Psalm 30:2 (NKJV)

The LORD is my strength and shield. I trust him with all my heart. He helps me, and my heart is filled with joy. I burst out in songs of thanksgiving.
 —*Psalm 28:7 (NLT)*

Where is another God like you, who pardons the guilt of the remnant, overlooking the sins of his special people? You will not stay angry with your people forever, because you delight in showing unfailing love. Once again you will have compassion on us. You will trample our sins under your feet and throw them into the depths of the ocean!
 —*Micah 7:18–19 (NLT)*

Praise the LORD, O my soul, and forget not all his benefits—who forgives all your sins and heals all your diseases.
 —*Psalm 103:2–3 (NIV)*

How great is your goodness, which you have stored up for those who fear you, which you bestow in the sight of men on those who take refuge in you.
—*Psalm 31:19 (NIV)*

He alone is your God, the only one who is worthy of your praise, the one who has done these mighty miracles that you have seen with your own eyes.
—*Deuteronomy 10:21 (NLT)*

Then you will say, "Praise the Lord! Worship his name! Tell all people about the things he has done!" Sing songs of praise about the Lord! Why? Because he has done great things! Spread this news about God through the whole world. Let all people know these things.
—*Isaiah 12:4–5 (ERV)*

Blessed be the God and Father of
our Lord Jesus Christ, the Father of
mercies and God of all comfort, who
comforts us in all our tribulation, that
we may be able to comfort those who
are in any trouble, with the comfort
with which we ourselves are comforted
by God.

—2 *Corinthians 1:3–4 (NKJV)*

[David] sang: "The LORD is my rock,
my fortress, and my savior; my God is
my rock, in whom I find protection. He
is my shield, the power that saves me,
and my place of safety. He is my refuge,
my savior, the one who saves me from
violence. I called on the LORD, who is
worthy of praise, and he saved me from
my enemies."

—2 *Samuel 22:2–4 (NLT)*

Then they cried to the LORD in their trouble, and he saved them from their distress. He sent forth his word and healed them; he rescued them from the grave. Let them give thanks to the LORD for his unfailing love and his wonderful deeds for men.

—*Psalm 107:19–21 (NIV)*

Praise the LORD! Praise God in his sanctuary; praise him in his mighty heaven! Praise him for his mighty works; praise his unequaled greatness! Praise him with a blast of the ram's horn; praise him with the lyre and harp! Praise him with the tambourine and dancing; praise him with strings and flutes! Praise him with a clash of cymbals; praise him with loud clanging cymbals. Let everything that breathes sing praises to the LORD! Praise the LORD!

—*Psalm 150:1–6 (NLT)*

God, your kindness makes me very happy. You have seen my suffering. You know about the troubles I have.

—*Psalm 31:7 (ERV)*

My Master, use this hard time to make my spirit live again. Help my spirit become strong and healthy. Help me become well! Help me live again! . . . Dead people don't sing praises to you. People in Sheol don't praise you. Dead people don't trust you to help them. They go into a hole in the ground, and never speak again. People that are alive—like me today—are the people that praise you. A father should tell his children that you can be trusted.

—*Isaiah 38:16, 18–19 (ERV)*

In this manner, therefore, pray: Our Father in heaven, hallowed be Your name. Your kingdom come. Your will be done on earth as it is in heaven. Give us this day our daily bread. And forgive us our debts, as we forgive our debtors. And do not lead us into temptation, but deliver us from the evil one. For Yours is the kingdom and the power and the glory forever. Amen.

—Matthew 6:9–13 (NKJV)